NEW YORK

SUSAN BERNSTEIN

MALLARD PRESS

First published in the United States of
America in 1992 by The Mallard Press
Mallard Press and its accompanying design
and logo are trademarks of BDD Promotional
Book Company, Inc.

ISBN 0-7924-5659-9

Printed in Hong Kong

Photo Credits

Susan Bernstein: 14 (top), 15, 20, 21, 22-23,
    24 (top), 25, 37, 40, 41, 46, 47, 64, 72-73,
    76, 79, 80, 86, 88-89, 90, 91, 95.
Joe DiMaggio/JoAnne Kalish: 7, 9, 10, 14
    (bottom), 16-17, 24 (bottom), 45, 55,
    56-57, 58, 59, 60-61, 62, 68, 71, 78, 83, 84-
    85, 94.
Audrey Gibson: 2, 54, 63, 82.
Mark Gibson: 4-5, 19, 70, 81, 96.
New England Stock Photography: Alan L.
    Detrick: 42-43, 74-75; Mario DiRosa: 27,
    35, 38, 87, 92, 93; Travis Evans: 77;
    Spencer Grant: 18, 48-49; Tony LaGruth:
    1, 6, 8, 11, 12-13; Clark Linehan Photography:
    44; Bill Melton: 50; Barbara L. Moore: 51;
    Margo Taussig Pinkerton: 26, 28-29, 30, 31,
    32, 33, 34, 36, 39, 65, 66-67, 69.
Rainbow: Dan McCoy 52, 53.

Acknowledgments

The author would like to thank the following
people who have helped in the preparation of
this book: Barbara Thrasher, who edited it;
Rita Longabucco, who did the picture research;
and Don Longabucco, who designed it.

To my parents

Page 1: The building of the World Trade Towers had a dramatic impact on the Lower Manhattan skyline. Rising 1,350 feet, the towers now dominate the cityscape.

Page 2: A bird's-eye view of Central Park and the impressive buildings that line Central Park West. Included on that street are the American Museum of Natural History and the luxury apartment building called the Dakota.

Below: The glittering cityscape of Manhattan. Surrounded by waterways, Manhattan offers many panoramic views.

Contents

Introduction

New York City is a most beguiling place. As one of the most exciting cities in the world, it defies easy descriptions and simple explanations. Though many people do not think of New York City as historic, especially in comparison to other cities in the United States, its history has affected its character in ways that continue to this day. New York was founded in pursuit of wealth and not, as other East Coast communities were, for religious reasons. Because of New York's secular goal, the city attracted a widely diverse population. Early in its history, Father Jogues, a French Jesuit missionary to the Mohawk Indians, noted 18 nationalities in this colony of less than 1,000. Perhaps it is the lure of riches and power, coupled with a historic tolerance for peoples of different cultures and backgrounds, that still compels native New Yorkers and visitors alike.

It is impossible to visit here and not be affected by the ambient energy of the city. This vitality inspires New Yorkers, who thrive upon the tangible sense that anything is possible here.

The freedom and anonymity possible in New York allow it also to be a city of excesses. There is no doubt that the Big Apple's problems are often as large as its rewards. Yet those who live and work here make the trade-off willingly. Limousines carrying well-heeled passengers rush along streets where homeless people huddle; talented street musicians entertain passers-by while others perform in world renowned concert halls; elegant mansions grace Fifth Avenue while decrepit tenement buildings still house the city's latest immigrants in Chinatown — thousands of contrasts and extremes can be seen in just one day in New York.

The ambitions and economic prosperity of New York's inhabitants have made their mark on the very look of the city. With the constant building and rebuilding, very little remains of its early structures. Yet many famous landmarks — Brooklyn Bridge, the Empire State Building and Carnegie Hall, for example — are imbued with a spirit of optimism, progress and culture. The fact that the Empire State Building, Rockefeller Center and the Chrysler Building were built during the height of the Depression underscores the gritty determination of those who shaped the city. Through prosperous and troubled times, New York resonates with an energy uniquely its own.

Left: The majestic Empire State Building dominates the distinctive skyline of mid-Manhattan.

Above: The Brooklyn Bridge (1867-83) is still one of the most picturesque bridges of New York. As a symbol of the ingenuity and progressive spirit of America, it is both an engineering feat and a structure of artistic beauty.

Lower Manhattan

Within the confines of Lower Manhattan many of the city's extremes coexist in close proximity. From the spectacular views of the prosperous financial district to the tenement dwelling in several ethnic enclaves, Lower Manhattan presents a study of contrasts.

The southern tip of Manhattan is where New York City began. Early settlers came by sea to make their fortunes in the New World. Throughout the nineteenth century people still arrived by boat, though the majestic sight of the Statue of Liberty and the screening procedures of Ellis Island greeted these newer immigrants.

First and foremost New York is a port city whose waterfront is still one of its vital resources. These ties to the sea are experienced most clearly at the South Street Seaport. In the nineteenth century trade with the world beyond centered in this docking area, where goods also arrived from the Midwest shipped via the Erie Canal and the Hudson River. The seaport fell into disuse for decades, but today its appealing renovation lures many visitors with an array of attractions: fine dining, authentic tall ships lining the dock, historic Schermerhorn Row, the Fulton Fish Market, and free jazz concerts. This area balances its commercial aspects with its historic significance, making it an important sight to see. A short distance north of the Seaport the celebrated Brooklyn Bridge spans the East River. From its pedestrian walkway a view of the harbor, backed by a spectacular city skyline, can be glimpsed.

Rising buildings and narrow, twisting streets distinguish the financial district, forming the area into dramatic canyons. During the week thousands of day workers fill the streets, busily moving from Wall Street and the New York Stock Exchange to their offices in the sleek World Trade Towers or the monumental Citibank Building.

To the Northeast, another area of Lower Manhattan retains historical significance. while playing a major role in contemporary city life. The civic center, where the city government and municipal buildings are located, orchestrates essential municipal functions. City Hall (1802-11) is an elegant cross of French Renaissance detail and Federal form. It has become the traditional end for Broadway tickertape parades.

Lower Manhattan's financial and governmental areas find their counterpart in the region's residential ethnic neighborhoods: the Lower East Side, Little Italy and Chinatown. The Lower East Side is one of Manhattan's least alluring neighborhoods, an area that toward the end of the last century became an insular ghetto for more than a million Jewish immigrants. This enclave is about 25 percent Jewish now (the rest is largely Hispanic and Chinese), but remnants of its Jewish identity still exist: synagogues, delicatessens, a kosher winery, and bargain street shopping. On Sundays as the Orchard Street Market swells with bargain-hunters, the area seems to regain its former vitality.

Though the Chinese now own and live in much of Little Italy, the enclave still retains its Italian character. Mulberry Street, the heart of Little Italy, is crowded with restaurants, cafes, bakeries and neighborhood food stores. The area is at its liveliest during the annual Festa di San Gennaro, when Mulberry Street becomes a sea of people and food stalls.

Chinatown is a truly thriving ethnic neighborhood with nearly 100,000 residents — almost half of New York's Chinese population. Though faced with overcrowding, poverty, and physical deterioration, it has one of the lowest official crime rates and highest employment rates of any neighborhood. The bustling streets with vegetable markets displaying exotic merchandise and the many busy restaurants reflect the vitality and hopefulness of the area's residents. The rich diversity of Lower Manhattan's ethnic neighborhoods lends color and contrast to the birthplace of the city.

Page 9

Left: *The Manhattan skyline forms a modern backdrop to historic Ellis Island. In the foreground is the Wall of Honor, inscribed with the names of many Ellis Island immigrants.*

Above: *Viewed from the Staten Island Ferry, the Lower Manhattan skyline seems to rise out of the sea.*

Above: *Perhaps the most famous statue in America, here the Statue of Liberty stands amidst the grand fireworks display during the patriotic celebration of its centennial in 1986.*

Right: *The Great Hall on Ellis Island processed more than 16 million immigrants over a 60-year period, before they could reach Manhattan. More than 40 percent of Americans living today are descended from these immigrants.*

Overleaf: *A view from Brooklyn of the South Street Seaport's Pier 17, a popular evening spot. The World Trade Towers rise in the background.*

Left: Schermerhorn Row at the South Street Seaport is one of the best remaining Federal warehouse groupings in America. Built in 1811, these buildings have been given new life with the renovation of the Seaport.

Below: The masts of the tall ships docked at the Seaport form a contrast to the modern, reflective skyscrapers in the background.

Right: A festive atmosphere prevails at the South Street Seaport when free concerts are held. Here performers entertain with a backdrop of tall ships.

Overleaf: Next door to the Seaport is the Fulton Fish Market, where brisk business is conducted among the fish-mongers; usually it's at full swing around 4 a.m.

Above: The awesome Gothic-arched towers of the Brooklyn Bridge rise 268 feet from the river below. The elevated pedestrian promenade offers majestic views of Manhattan's skyline, the river, and the sweeping web of the bridge's supporting cables.

Above: The Staten Island Ferry provides perhaps the world's best short ocean voyage. For 50 cents, the hour-and-a-half boat tour of New York's Upper Bay offers spectacular views of the city and the Statue of Liberty.

Page 20: The Lower East Side's history as a Jewish enclave is evident by the store signs in Hebrew. Though the area's residents are more ethnically mixed now, one can still see how Jewish immigrants shaped this neighborhood.

Page 21: The Orchard Street Market on the Lower East Side draws bargain shoppers from all over New York on Sundays.

Pages 22-23: Mulberry Street is the heart of Little Italy, a colorful area filled with fine restaurants, pastry shops, and Italian food markets. Many visitors come here for the carnival-like Feast of San Gennaro held in September.

Left top: *Porcelain vases made in China colorfully decorate a street in Chinatown.*

Left: *New Year's celebrations in Chinatown bring out masked dragon dancers and firecracker explosions.*

Above: *The bustling streets of Chinatown on a Sunday afternoon. Chinatown is a vibrant community that continues to expand while other ethnic neighborhoods fade.*

SoHo and Greenwich Village

SoHo, an acronym for SOuth of HOuston Street, was "discovered" in the 1960s by both artists and preservationists. The artists found cheap and spacious housing in studio and loft apartments carved out of former industrial buildings. The preservationists were attracted by the buildings' exteriors; this area contains the world's largest concentration of cast iron buildings.

By the 1970s SoHo real estate was booming. Art dealers moved in and film directors used the area in movies to portray the ultimate in trendy neighborhoods. By the 1980s galleries, chic shops and cafes made SoHo a desirable residential area. Unable to afford skyrocketing rents, most of the artists moved out.

North of SoHo, Greenwich Village is a concentration of diversity. From its street plan to its architecture to the people who reside here, the Village has been molded by the idiosyncracies of its unique heritage. Greenwich Village began as a small Algonquin settlement. The Dutch quickly dispatched the native population and divided the land into large farms. Wealthy individuals such as Aaron Burr settled in the Village during the 1700s. As the city expanded northward and people fled the yellow fever epidemics of the 1800s, the Village's large estates were broken up and sold as building lots. Around the turn of the century the Village became a haven for the radical and avant-garde in America. Low rents

and freedom from Victorian mores attracted political activists such as Max Eastman; playwrights and performers such as Eugene O'Neill, Edna St. Vincent Millay, and Bette Davis; writers such as Theodore Dreiser and John Dos Passos; and poets such as e.e. cummings, Hart Crane, and Marianne Moore. Many others followed until rising rents drove out the struggling artists. Yet despite the fact that the Village is no longer bohemian, its mystique still endures.

The Village's distinctive street pattern escaped much of the grid plan imposed upon the rest of Manhattan. A pleasant tree-lined street may curve sharply in one drection for no apparent reason. Streets and properties here often follow the irregular lines of past farms, streams or Indian paths. These twists and alleys, along with the area's eclectic architecture, add to the Village's charm.

The Village is home to many professionals who enjoy the sense of community the area affords, and in keeping with its long-standing tolerance, the Village is also home to a sizable gay community. Though struggling artists have moved away in search of more reasonable housing, and though the coffeehouses that were made famous by the Beat writers of the 1950s are now more for the tourists than for literary figures, the Village still exudes a spirit and vibrancy that makes it anything but colorless.

Left: The redbrick Puck Building (1885) in SoHo was home to the nineteenth-century satirical magazine Puck. *A gilded statue of Shakespeare's Puck appears above the entrance.*

Above: Washington Arch, at the beginning of Fifth Avenue, bathed in floodlights in this eye-catching view. The Arch was built in 1892 to commemorate Washington's inauguration 100 years earlier.

Overleaf: Outdoor cafes are especially popular in Greenwich Village. Patrons can enjoy a meal and still people-watch at the same time.

Page 30: Chess games are only one of the activities in Washington Square Park. Known for its sometimes frenetic energy, the park accommodates joggers, musicians, political activists, and NYU students.

Page 31: New York University, the nation's largest private university, draws students to Greenwich Village. NYU owns much of the real estate around Washington Square.

Above: *The Manhattan Brewing Company,
a unique meeting place located in SoHo,
brews its own beer for its clientele.*

Above: *This popular coffeehouse on Bleecker Street, the main street of the Village, was made famous by the Beat writers of the 1950s.*

Page 34: *Cooper Union Foundation Building (1859) was founded to provide a tuition-free, technical education to the working class. Its Great Hall was the site of Abraham Lincoln's "Might Makes Right" speech of 1860. The subway kiosk in the foreground is a beautiful replica of the original.*

Page 35: *What was once a narrow carriageway became 75 1/2 Bedford Street, the narrowest house in the Village and, for a short time, the home of poet Edna St. Vincent Millay. Next door (right) is the Isaac-Hendricks House, built in 1799.*

Above: The Washington Mews is a private, cobblestoned street lined on one side by the former stables of the houses of The Row.

Right: The Row, a grouping of Federal-styled townhouses that line Washington Square North, recalls the staid atmosphere of Henry James's novel, **Washington Square.** *Here is one of the redbrick houses, which retains its original look.*

Page 38: Craft and jewelry vendors sell their wares on the streets in Greenwich Village.

Page 39: Union Square Park, once known for its political rallies, fell upon hard times when it became a gathering place for drug dealers. Fortunately, in recent times farmer's markets such as this one are helping residents reclaim the area.

Midtown

Midtown is the center of the city. Encompassing most of the city's hotels, major railroad and bus stations, the largest stores, the main library and post office, the theater district, the convention center, and a number of New York City's famed landmarks, Midtown has something to offer everyone.

Unlike Manhattan below 14th Street, Midtown (and above) is laid out in a gridiron street system, with Fifth Avenue as the dividing line between the East Side and the West Side. Although traditionally the East Side has maintained a reputation for being wealthy and chic, and the West Side has tended toward shabbiness, today these distinctions have blurred. Characterized by its corporate businesses, the East Side receives its many thousands of commuters at Penn Station, the Port Authority Bus Terminal, or the Beaux Arts masterpiece known as Grand Central Station. Several avenues on the East Side have their own unique image.

Fifth Avenue, the artery of Midtown, has become synonymous with opulence and sophistication. Though the stores may be a bit too pricey to shop in, Fifth Avenue also offers some of the city's best architecture. The Empire State Building (1931) is the most evocative symbol of the city. Once the world's tallest building, it boasts fine Art Deco detailing, and offers panoramic views from its observation deck. Beaux Arts architecture finds its expression further north on Fifth Avenue, in the Main Branch of the Public Library. The nation's third largest reference library, it houses more than 63 miles of shelves.

At Fifth Avenue between 50th and 51st streets resides another of Manhattan's famous landmarks: the Gothic Revival St. Patrick's Cathedral (1878), the seat of the Roman Catholic Archdiocese of New York. To the West stretches Rockefeller Center, a large complex of commercial buildings, plazas, an ice skating rink in winter, underground pedestrian walkways, and Radio City Music Hall.

The West Side is known for its garment district, theater district and Times Square. The garment district produces about three-quarters of all women's and children's clothing made in the U.S., but you'd never know it from the look of the area. Only the racks of clothes being wheeled across the streets and the usually congested traffic of the area give some hint as to the business being conducted.

Times Square, also known as the Crossroads of the World, is an energy center that is as exciting and glittering as it is seedy and dirty. Legitimate Broadway theaters share the area with X-rated movie houses. Hundreds of thousands of revelers gather here each New Year's Eve to celebrate.

Further uptown is Carnegie Hall, world renowned for its superb acoustics. Such illustrious conductors and performers as Tchaikovsky, Toscanini, Rubinstein and Horowitz have graced its stage. Saved from demolition in the 1960s when violinist Isaac Stern and other performers fought to preserve it, the Hall remains a vital part of the city's cultural heritage that finds much of its expression in Midtown's vast array of arts institutions.

Left: *A steady stream of traffic negotiates Park Avenue in this nighttime view. Park Avenue became a preferred address once the railroad yards and tracks leading into Grand Central went underground. The Helmsley Building is lit on the right.*

Above: *Radio City Music Hall, America's third largest indoor theater and an Art Deco gem, is the ultimate expression of 1930s luxury. Seasonal shows featuring the leggy Rockettes always delight audiences.*

Overleaf: *A view of Midtown from the World Trade Center. Several Midtown landmarks stand out, lighting the night sky: the Empire State Building, the Chrysler Building and the Citicorp Building.*

Left: This view of geometric patterns in windows is from the Jacob Javits Convention Center (1986).

Above: The famous World War II aircraft carrier, The Intrepid, permanently docked on the West Side, now houses the Sea-Air-Space Museum.

—45—

Above: *This is a typical crowded scene of Rockefeller Center during the Christmas season. People flock here to see the giant Christmas tree, go ice skating or do some last-minute shopping.*

Right: *The statue of Atlas faces St. Patrick's Cathedral, the largest Catholic cathedral in America. St. Patrick's is a symbol of the collective success of New York's immigrant Irish Catholic population.*

Overleaf: *With the Manhattan Bridge in the foreground, the Midtown Manhattan skyline takes on a sunset glow.*

Page 50: *The quintessential building of New York City, the Empire State Building. Its observation decks on the 86th and 102nd floors offer incredible views of the Big Apple, which spreads out in all directions.*

Page 51: *The Chrysler Building (1930) is probably New Yorkers' favorite building. This Art Deco delight was for a very short time the tallest building in the world. From the African marble and chrome steel of the lobby to the jutting gargoyles and arched stainless steel crown, this building adds a bit of fun to the city's skyline.*

Above and right: Fifth Avenue – the artery of Midtown – harbors many elegant shops where sophisticated fashion may be found. Prosperous New Yorkers come here to shop at some of the world's finest stores.

GLOOM · OF · NIGHT · ST · YS · THESE · COURIERS · FROM · THE · SWIFT · CO

Left: *A fascinating juxtaposition with St. Bartholomew's Church reflected off the sleek exterior of the ITT Building.*

Above: *Located on Eighth Avenue, the U.S. General Post Office (1910-13) is an imposing structure with 20 large Corinthian columns and the now familiar motto of the post office inscribed on the entire length of the building.*

Overleaf: *Grand Central Terminal has been a symbol of New York since its completion in 1913. It accommodates a huge network of commuter railroads and the needs of the 400,000 people who use it every day. This interior view shows the mastery of space in the Beaux Arts style.*

Left: The New York Public Library's Main Branch on Fifth Avenue is one of the world's top research institutions. Free tours of its lavish interior and ongoing exhibits are held throughout the building.

Right: Built on a site that allows it to be viewed in its entirety from two sides, Fifth Avenue's Plaza Hotel is known for its lovely facade and its social history. The Plaza has witnessed many showy events and attracted such guests as Mark Twain, F. Scott Fitzgerald and Cary Grant, and no doubt the entire New York Social Register.

Overleaf: Carnegie Hall opened in 1891 with Peter Ilich Tchaikovsky as guest conductor. The Hall has hosted illustrious conductors, performers and symphonies on its acoustically renowned stage, from Arturo Toscanini to Benny Goodman.

Page 62: The unusual Flatiron Building (1902) was built on a triangular lot and thus its rounded front point is only six feet wide. For years it symbolized the dramatic new age of skyscrapers.

Page 63: The United Nations Headquarters is located on the East River on 18 beautifully landscaped acres.

ANDREW CARNEGIE

Central Park and Upper Manhattan

One of New York City's best known and well used sites is Central Park. The idea for a city-owned public space was proposed by poet William Cullen Bryant and landscape planner Andrew Jackson Downing in the 1850s. An 843-acre site was selected in the middle of Manhattan, and a design competition was held. The plan submitted by Frederick Law Olmsted and Calvert Vaux called for a park that appeared so natural it would belie the fact that every inch was planned and created by man. The area, occupied at the time by about 5,000 squatters along with assorted farm animals, was a swampy foul-smelling place. But Central Park has become the city's backyard. To the many who use its recreational fields, go rowboating, or just picnic here, the park is what makes living in Manhattan tolerable.

Central Park lies between the Upper East Side and the Upper West Side. Both sides are residential areas but each has a character all its own. The Upper East Side, with its old opulent mansions, ivy-covered townhouses and door-men apartment buildings, is home to some of New York's wealthiest people. Art galleries and fine boutiques abound. Fifth Avenue between 82nd and 104th streets is known as the Museum Mile and it includes the Metropolitan Museum of Art (the Met), which houses a permanent collection of 3.3 million works of art from all over the world; Frank Lloyd Wright's Guggenheim Museum, one of the city's most unique buildings; and others such as the Cooper Hewitt Museum, the Jewish Museum, the Museum of the City of New York, and El Museo del Barrio.

The Upper West Side has a reputation for harboring New Yorkers of artistic temperaments.

Many who live here perform or take classes at Lincoln Center for the Performing Arts. The 12-acre complex is a cultural mecca that contains the New York State Theater, The Metropolitan Opera House, Avery Fisher Music Hall, Vivian Beaumont Theater, Library and Museum of Performing Arts, and the Julliard School. The West Side is less refined than its eastern counterpart, though the well-heeled reside here too, as the luxury apartment buildings along Central Park West attest. However, much of the area is a residential mix with pockets of slum areas.

Further north, on the southern border of Harlem, is the immense Cathedral Church of St. John the Divine. Begun in 1892, it is still only about two-thirds finished, and local residents trained by English stonemasons continue the work. When completed it will be the largest cathedral in the world. Another New York landmark in the vicinity is Columbia University, one of the country's oldest, largest, and wealthiest institutions.

In upper Manhattan sprawls Harlem, the center for black American life and culture for most of this century. In the 1920s an impressive number of talented black artists, writers and musicians gathered here, creating what has been called the "Harlem Renaissance." Hard times from the Depression through the unrest of the 1960s turned Harlem into a seething ghetto. But recently signs of Harlem's revitalization include the restoration of the Apollo Theatre, and renovation of some fine brownstones which now share the area with burnt-out houses and vacant lots. Home to many, and offering leisure activities to many more, upper Manhattan and Central Park represent a slice of city life.

Left: The American Museum of Natural History has an amazing collection of 37 million artifacts. From the halls of dinosaur skeletons to the Star of India, the largest blue sapphire in the world, the Museum has something of interest to everybody.

Above: There are many out-of-the-ordinary jobs in New York, which lend themselves to humorous scenes. Here a dogsitter takes her numerous charges for a walk on the Upper East Side.

Overleaf: East 69th Street between Lexington and Third avenues is a reminder of the vital role horses played in New York's history. These buildings were formerly carriage houses and stables.

Above: Central Park looks like this most weekends in the summer. The park is an oasis of green for city dwellers; a much needed touch of country living.

Right: Dining on the outdoor terrace of the fanciful and busy Tavern on the Green. Originally built as a sheepfold for sheep pastured on the meadows in Central Park, it was converted into a restaurant in the 1930s.

Left: *The luminous Metropolitan Opera House at Lincoln Center for the Performing Arts is just one of the reasons why New York is the cultural capital of America.*

Above: *Street festivals are held all over Manhattan, and nothing is more synonymous with these festivals than food. Local restaurants and street vendors set up stalls offering a most diversified menu.*

Overleaf: *Rising out of the shabby surrounding neighborhood north of Central Park is the unfinished Gothic Cathedral Church of St. John the Divine. Though only two-thirds completed, this cathedral is the largest in the world.*

Pages 74-75: *Frank Lloyd Wright's controversial Guggenheim Museum incorporates a unique spiral design with a spiral ramp cantilevered out from its inside walls. The Museum houses modern art from the Impressionist period to the present.*

Left: The Metropolitan Museum of Art is the largest art museum in the Western Hemisphere. Although the Met exhibits only part of its collection, it offers more than what can be realistically seen in one outing.

Above: *The Cloisters, the only branch of the Metropolitan Museum of Art, is located in Fort Tryon Park on Manhattan's northernmost tip. The Cloisters houses much of the Met's medieval collection and includes five medieval European cloisters, a twelfth-century chapter house, and many more treasures.*

Above: *The staff of Sylvia's, a renowned soul food restaurant in Harlem. This is the place to go if you're craving some authentic southern cooking.*

Above: *Low Memorial Library (1895-97) was the first building erected on Columbia University's new uptown campus. This was a focal point of demonstrations during the Vietnam War.*

Images

Oftentimes a single image can convey a tangible feeling about a place. New York City can easily be experienced as a visual explosion of colors and movement. But much of the essence of Manhattan exists beyond the famous landmarks and bustling crowds. For it is the city's quiet, often elusive scenes that can truly touch us. These images can be humorous, poignant, meditative, ironic, or resonate with the past. Just as some images recall the past — such as a richly ornamented and brightly painted tenement apartment building — others bring the past to life — such as the horse-drawn hansom cab carrying passengers through Central Park and the streets of New York. And everywhere there are scenes that capture the flavor of everyday life in the city — food vendors setting up for business on street corners, or a fireman adding a bit more gloss to the brilliant red door of the firehouse.

It is easy to be overwhelmed by the hectic pace and the noise of the city, and to overlook the images that shape its character. New York City offers countless such moments to all who are willing to look beyond the surface. Perhaps more often than not, it is these types of images that stand out most in the minds of New Yorkers and visitors alike.

Left: Sometimes you can find a bit of solitude in the Big Apple.

Above: *This fireman is making sure that the brilliant red door of the firehouse keeps its high lustre.*

Overleaf: *A smart-looking marching band brings music and pageantry to one of New York City's many parades.*

Above: What would a parade be without clowns? These New Yorkers in costume await their turn to join the procession.

Above: *A family at an outdoor Mexican cafe adds a touch of humor as the cool baby dons his shades.*

Overleaf: *Old-style tenement buildings with elaborate iron work and fire escapes line some of the streets of Lower Manhattan.*

Above: First looks can be deceiving. This mural of a subway car with furry riders is actually painted on the side of a building.

Right: The bright redbrick tenement building with green trim and ornamented fire escape adds a dash of color to the neighborhood.

Page 92: Horses are still part of the New York scene, as hansom cabs carry passengers through the streets.

Page 93: Scenes that might seem a bit unusual elsewhere are typical in New York. A man with his radio crew speaks on the telephone in the middle of the street.

Above: *A commonplace sight all around New York: food vendors on street corners.*

Right: *This restaurant on the Lower East Side touts its ethnic fare.*

Page 96: *This colorful tugboat is docked next to the tall ships at the South Street Seaport.*